Junior Science
sliding and rolling

Terry Jennings

Illustrations by David Anstey
Gloucester Press
New York · London · Toronto · Sydney

About this book

You can learn many things about sliding and rolling in this book. There are lots of activities and experiments for you to try. You can find out why some shapes slide and others roll, what makes things slide and roll easily, how to make a roller and much more.

First published in the
United States in 1989 by
Gloucester Press
387 Park Avenue South
New York, NY 10016

ISBN 0 531 17130 2

Library of Congress Catalog
Card Number: 88-83100

This book was designed and produced by BLA
Publishing Limited, TR House, Christopher
Road, East Grinstead, Sussex, England.
A member of the Ling Kee Group
London Hong Kong Taipei Singapore New York

Printed in Spain by Heraclio Fournier, S.A.

Stand a can of sand on a sloping piece of wood. Push the can gently so it slides down the slope.

Now lay the can down at the top of the slope and let it go. The can will roll down the slope. It will roll further than it slid.

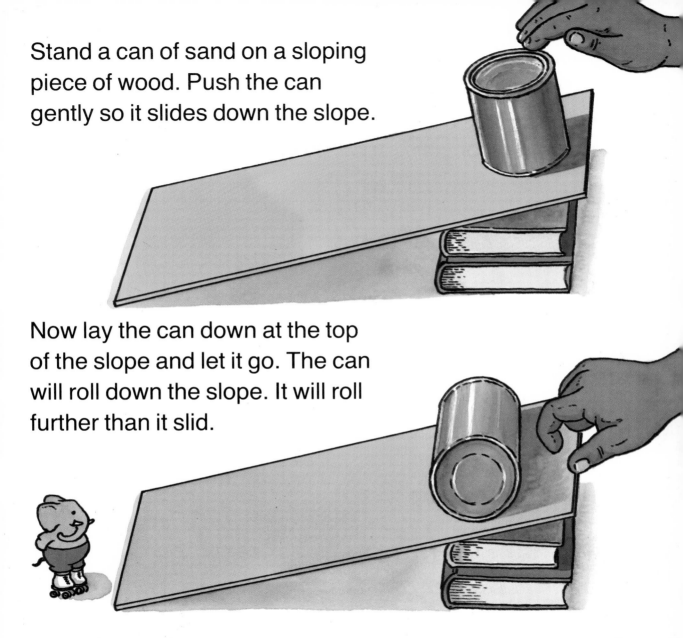

3

These pictures show things
that are sliding and rolling. The sled and boat are
sliding. The go-cart and barrel are rolling. The
things that slide have a flat surface, and the things
that roll have a round surface touching the ground.

4

We can move things by pushing or pulling. In the pictures the sled and go-cart are being pulled, while the barrel and boat are being pushed.

5

This girl has a heavy box. She tried to push it across the floor. The box and the floor are rough. The box was hard to push because it did not slide easily.

This boy also has a heavy box. But his box is on wheels. His box is much easier to push. Rolling is easier than sliding over bumps. The girl could fix the wheels onto her box to make it easier to push.

6

These people are using rollers to move a heavy chest. The chest moves easily over the two rollers. Then another roller is put in front. Soon the chest moves off the back roller. Then this roller is put in front again.

8

Put a plank of wood on a smooth floor and put a book under one end of the plank. The plank will make a slope. Let a toy truck roll down the slope and on to the floor. Measure how far the truck rolls across the floor.

Now put two books under the plank and let the truck roll down the slope again. Measure how far it rolls. The truck will roll further than it did before. If you put the plank on a rug the truck will not roll as far.

9

Make a roller from a spool. Take a rubber band, two cardboard rings, a paper clip and a popsicle stick. Put the roller together like this.

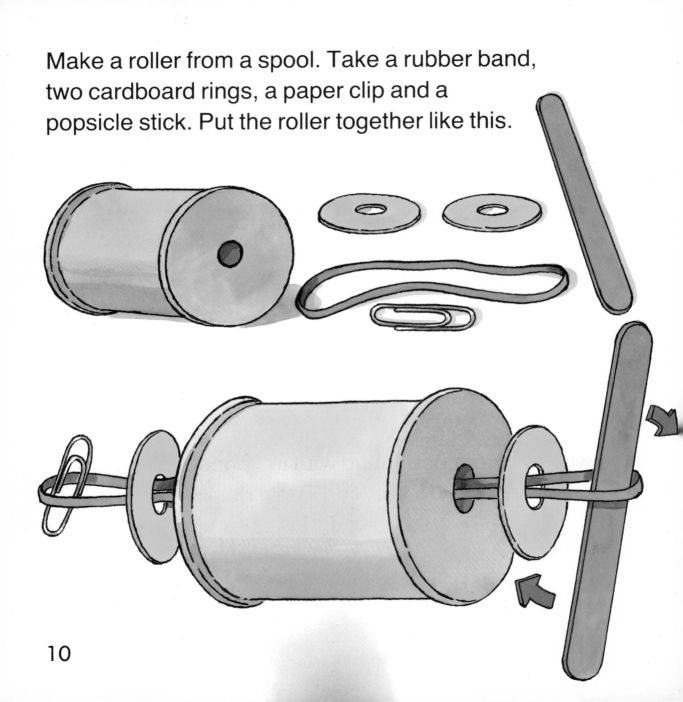

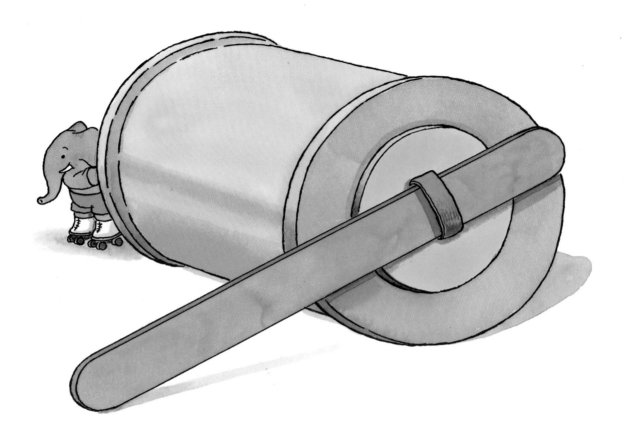

Now wind up the rubber band with the popsicle stick
and put the roller on the carpet. The roller will roll
across the carpet. Wind up the rubber band again
and put the roller on a smooth floor. The roller will
not roll as far this time because it cannot grip the
floor as well.

Take an empty can and roll it across the floor. It will roll a long way. Stick some modeling clay on the inside of the can and put the lid back on. Now, it will now not roll as far.

The can in the picture is on a slope. It is not rolling because one side is full of modeling clay.

This boy is wearing ice skates. He likes to skate on the ice. The girl is wearing roller skates. She likes to skate on the playground. The boy is sliding and the girl is rolling. The boy could not skate on the playground, and the girl could not skate on the ice.

Put a large sheet of wood on a table. Tie a piece of string to a small box and tie a small paper cup to the other end of the string. Put the box on the table like this and mark where the edge of the box is. Now put marbles in the cup, one at a time.

When there are a few marbles in the paper cup, the box will slide. Empty the cup and put the box back to where it had started from. Put some modeling clay in the box. Now more marbles will be needed in the cup to make the box slide.

Take another box and tie a paper cup to it. Put marbles in the cup until the box begins to slide. See how many marbles you need.

Next stick a piece of sandpaper on the bottom of the box.

Now put marbles in the cup to make the box slide again. You will need more marbles to make the box slide with the rough sandpaper attached to the box. If you put a little water on the wood, you will need fewer marbles to make the box slide across the wet surface.

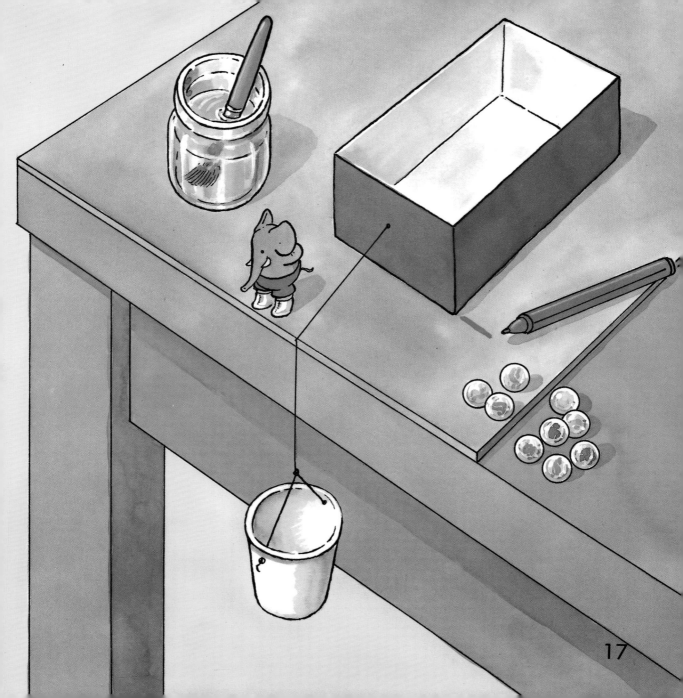

In the picture it is a cold and frosty morning. The boy is walking to school. There is ice on the path. The ice makes the path very slippery. It is hard for the boy to walk. He keeps slipping and sliding and soon falls over. Oily floors and wet floors are also slippery to walk on.

19

Wheels are round, but they do not always
roll. Sometimes car wheels slide. When
this happens the car skids. A car may skid
in the snow or when it has to stop quickly.

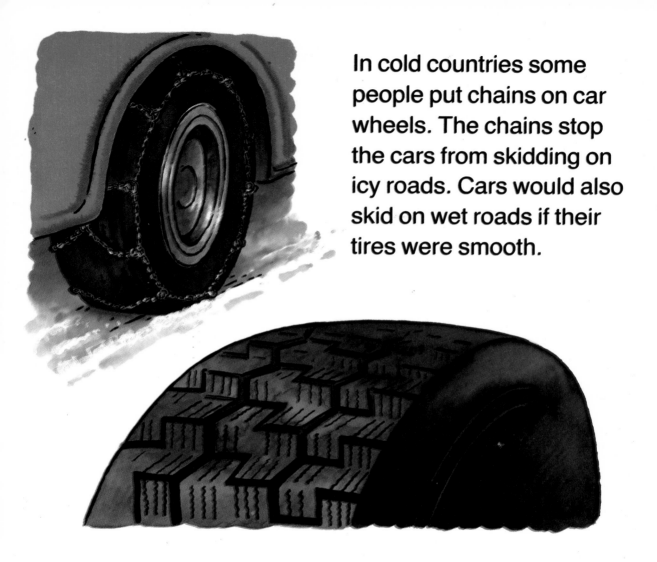

In cold countries some people put chains on car wheels. The chains stop the cars from skidding on icy roads. Cars would also skid on wet roads if their tires were smooth.

To stop a car skidding, its tires are like this. Then the tires can grip the road better.

Look at the picture. Some of the shapes will roll well,
like the sphere. Others will slide well, like the cube.
And others will both roll and slide, like the cylinder.

22

glossary

Here are the meanings of some words you may have used for the first time in this book.

grip: to take a firm hold of something.

plank: a long flat piece of wood.

roll: to turn over and over like a ball or a wheel running along the ground.

roller: a piece of wood, metal or plastic shaped like a cylinder.

skid: to slip or slide without meaning to.

slide: to slip smoothly over the surface of something.

slope: a line or surface that goes gradually upward or downward.

smooth: having a surface without any bumps that can be felt.

index

box 6, 14, 15, 16

bricks 6

can 3, 12

car 20, 21

chains 21

chest 7

clay 12, 15

floor 6, 9, 11

grip 21

ice 13, 18

ice skates 13

marbles 14, 15, 16

plank 9

push 3

road 21

roller 7, 10, 11

roller skates 13

sand 3

sandpaper 16

shape 4, 22

skid 20, 21

slope 3, 9, 12

smooth 6, 9, 11

snow 20

spool 10

table 14

tires 21

truck 9

wheels 6, 20, 21

wood 9, 14, 16